For all the Rylants, especially my mother, Leatrel

— C.R.

And for Lemuria, a voice in the wilderness

— B.M.

APPA

LACHIA

THE VOICES OF SLEEPING BIRDS

by Cynthia Rylant

Illustrated by Barry Moser

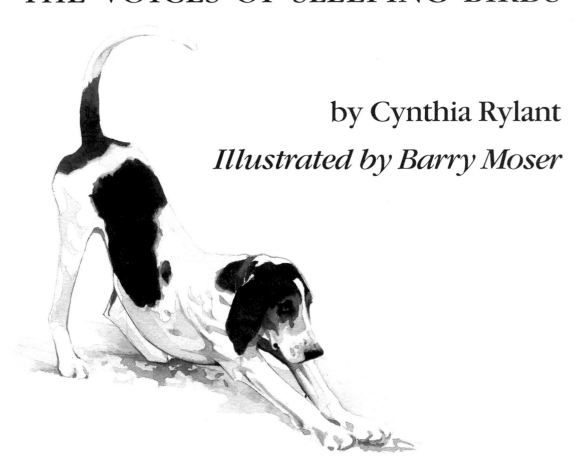

HARCOURT BRACE JOVANOVICH, PUBLISHERS

San Diego · New York · London

Text copyright © 1991 by Cynthia Rylant
Illustrations copyright © 1991 by Pennyroyal Press, Inc.

The quote opening this book is from "Knoxville: Summer 1915" reprinted by permission of
Grosset & Dunlap from *A Death in the Family* by James Agee, © 1957 by
The James Agee Trust, © renewed 1985 by Mia Agee.

Library of Congress Cataloging-in-Publication Data
Rylant, Cynthia.
Appalachia: the voices of sleeping birds/by Cynthia Rylant;
illustrated by Barry Moser. — 1st ed.
p.   cm.
ISBN 0-15-201605-8
1. Appalachian Region, Southern — Description and travel.
2. Appalachian Region, Southern — Social life and customs.
I. Title.
F217.A65R95 1991   90-36798
974'.009734 — dc20

First edition   A B C D E

Special thanks to Camilla Filancia

The pictures in this book were painted with transparent watercolors on paper
handmade for the Royal Watercolor Society in 1982 by J. Barcham Greene.
The calligraphy is the work of Reassurance Wunder.
The text type was set in ITC Garamond Book by Thompson Type, San Diego, California.
Color separations were made by Bright Arts, Ltd., Singapore.
Printed and bound by Tien Wah Press, Singapore
Production supervision by Warren Wallerstein and Ginger Boyer
Designed by Barry Moser

APPALACHIA

THE VOICES OF SLEEPING BIRDS

*O*N the rough wet grass of the back yard my father and mother have spread quilts. We all lie there, my mother, my father, my uncle, my aunt, and I too am lying there. First we were sitting up, then one of us lay down, and then we all lay down, on our stomachs, or on our sides, or on our backs, and they have kept on talking. They are not talking much, and the talk is quiet, of nothing in particular, of nothing at all in particular, of nothing at all. The stars are wide and alive, they seem each like a smile of great sweetness, and they seem very near. All my people are larger bodies than mine, quiet, with voices gentle and meaningless like the voices of sleeping birds. . . ."

JAMES AGEE
Knoxville: Summer 1915

IN A CERTAIN PART of
the country called Appalachia you will find dogs
named Prince or King living in little towns with
names like Coal City and Sally's Backbone. These
dogs run free, being country dogs, and their
legs are full of muscles from running rabbits up
mountains or from following boys who push
old bikes against the hill roads they call hollows.
These are mostly good dogs and can be trusted.

The owners of these dogs who live in
Appalachia have names like Mamie and Boyd and

1

Oley, and they probably have lived in Appalachia all of their lives. Many of them were born in coal camps in tiny houses which stood on poles and on the sides of which you could draw a face with your finger because coal dust had settled on their walls like snow. The owners of these dogs grew up more used to trees than sky and inside them had this feeling of mystery about the rest of the world they couldn't see because mountains came up so close to them and blocked their view like a person standing in a doorway. They weren't sure about going beyond these mountains, going until the land becomes flat or ocean, and so they stayed where they knew for sure how the sun would come up in the morning and set again at night.

The owners of these good dogs work pretty hard. Many of them are coal miners because the

3

mountains in Appalachia are full of coal which people want and if you are brave enough to travel two miles down into solid dark earth to get it, somebody will pay you money for your trouble. The men and women who mine the coal probably had fathers and grandfathers who were miners before them. Maybe some thought they didn't have any other choice but to be a miner, living in between or on the sides of these mountains, and seeing no way to go off and become doctors or teachers and having no wish to become soldiers.

Those who do go off, who find some way to become doctors or teachers, nearly always come back to the part of Appalachia where they grew up. They're never good at explaining why. Some will say they had brothers and sisters still here and they

5

missed them. But most will shake their heads and have a look on their faces like the look you see on dogs who wander home after being lost for a couple weeks and who search out that corner of the yard they knew they had to find again before they could get a good sleep.

Those who don't live in Appalachia and don't understand it sometimes make the mistake of calling these people "hillbillies." It isn't a good word for them. They probably would prefer "Appalachians." Like anyone else, they're sensitive about words.

The houses in Appalachia are as different as houses anywhere. Some are wood and some are brick. Some have real flowers in pots on the porch and some have plastic ones. Some have shiny new

cars parked in their driveways and some have only the parts of old cars parked in theirs. Most have running water inside the house, with sinks in their kitchens, washing machines in their basements, and pretty blue bathrooms. But a few still have no water pipes inside their houses and they carry their water from an old well or a creek over the hill and they wash themselves in metal tubs and build themselves wooden toilets in their back yards, which most of them call "outhouses."

Inside their homes you will see photographs on the walls, mostly of their children or their families from long ago. And you will see pretty things they have made hanging on these walls: clocks carved from wood, sometimes in the shape of their state, or wreaths made from corn husks.

9

Some will have pictures they bought at the department store when they went into town.

In their bedrooms there are usually one or two or three quilts somebody in the family made. In the winter these are on the bed, but usually not on top. And in the summer they stay folded up on shelves in small dark closets which smell of old wood and moth balls.

The good dogs who live in Appalachia are not allowed on these beds and most of them are not allowed in the house at all. They have their own houses.

The kitchens of these houses where Mamie or Boyd or Oley live almost always smell like fried bacon or chicken and on top of the stoves there are little plates of food with leftovers from

11

breakfast or lunch or supper and you can help your-self to a biscuit or maybe a piece of cornbread crumbled into a glass of buttermilk or some cold fried squash. What you don't eat up, the good dogs outside will get and they are happiest when it's the sausage gravy no one could finish.

Morning in these houses in Appalachia is quiet and full of light and the mountains out the window look new, like God made them just that day. Night in these houses is thick, the mountains wear heavy shawls of fog, and giant moths flap at the porch lights while cars cut through the dark hollows like burrowing moles.

If it is Sunday nearly everyone will go to church. Most of these Appalachians are Baptists but many are Methodists or Presbyterians and

13

some are Catholics. If the church is a Baptist church in the country you can count on people wearing their good clothes—women in dresses, men in suits and ties, and babies dressed up like pictures. There will be a lot of singing in that church and maybe some crying for joy and after the service people will linger in the yard, talking, till the women say it's time to eat, and they will go home and sit around a table spread with potatoes and beans and meat and good hot coffee or sweet iced tea and they will eat until they can eat no more except for the piece of lemon pound cake they saved some room for.

Sunday afternoon they will go to the houses of their relatives to visit and will sit around a kitchen table again, talking, or on the front porch. They

15

might do a little work for their mothers who live alone, carrying a big box to the shed for her or taking care of the nest of bees hiding near her basement door. Sunday night some of them will go to church again.

In the summer many of the women like to can. It seems their season. They sit on kitchen chairs on back porches and they talk of their lives while they snap beans or cut up cucumbers for pickling. It is a good way for them to catch up on things and to have time together, alone, for neither the children nor the men come around much when there is canning going on.

In the winter many of the men like to hunt, and this seems their season. They take off into the woods together, their good dogs running ahead,

17

and they hunt rabbit and sometimes deer and they talk about things and feel happy and free. If they shoot something, they bring it back home and skin it and cut it up and put it in their freezer to cook and eat later.

The children love all the seasons. They go down by the creek or into the woods or up the dirt roads with their good dogs and they feel more important than anything else in these Appalachian mountains, and probably they think often of God since they know the clouds and trees better than anyone. They have seen what God can do.

In summer if you walk the roads you will smell honeysuckle and the odors of cows and that gritty aroma dirt roads in the mountains send up your nose. The dogs will have a different smell every day.

19

The men and women and children who live in Appalachia have no sourness about them and though they are shy toward outsiders, they will wave to you if you drive by in your car whether they know your face or not. Most would probably rather not meet anyone new, but once they are used to you, you will find them bringing you bags of tomatoes from their gardens and sometimes a cherry cobbler. Most of them are thinkers, because these mountains inspire that, but they could never find the words to tell you of these thoughts they have. They talk to you of their corn or their cows instead and they keep the thoughts to themselves.

When they die, they will want the preacher at their church to say the words at their funeral and they will want to be buried in the Appalachian

Mountains with their families. They will want someone to put flowers on their graves on Memorial Day.

While they are living they will look forward to spring so they can go to the Southern States store and buy packages of seeds to plant: and they will look forward to summer so they can work outside among the sunflowers, repairing their fences: and they will look forward to fall so they can rock on their porches and stare toward shimmering painted mountains: and they will look forward to winter so they can build their fires and watch the hollows fill up with snow, safe till the next year begins, Prince or King running the mountains like all good dogs in Appalachia.

ABOUT THE AUTHOR

Cynthia Rylant was raised in Raleigh County, West Virginia, during the 1960s. Her family traces its roots back to the coal camps of 1920s rural Alabama. Her grandfather, Ferrell, worked in the mines of Alabama and West Virginia for forty-two years. He died of "black lung" disease at age seventy-two. Her mother, Leatrel, and her grandmother, Elda, live near the mouth of a hollow in Cool Ridge, West Virginia, which has been home to them for nearly forty years.

ABOUT THE ILLUSTRATOR

Barry Moser was raised in Hamilton County, Tennessee, during the 1940s and 1950s. His family's home was at the foot of Missionary Ridge in Chattanooga. Both his Grandfather Moser and his Grandfather Haggard ran grocery stores. In fact, the illustration on page 2 is based on a photograph of his brother, Tommy, standing on the porch of Grandpa Haggard's store. Moser often adapts photographs for his pictures, his own and others': the coon dog, for instance, was photographed by the artist in the spring of 1990 in Dawsonville, Georgia — the southernmost point in Appalachia. Some of the other illustrations were adapted from photographs taken by men and women who had earlier traveled and documented Appalachia: Ben Shahn, Walker Evans, Marion Post Wolcott, and Dorothea Lange.